John Adams
Speaks for Freedom

John Adams
Speaks for Freedom

written by
Deborah Hopkinson

illustrated by
Craig Orback

Aladdin

New York   London   Toronto   Sydney

For Andy, my own "Dearest Friend" —D. H.

For N. C. Wyeth, a giant among illustrators
and my artistic hero —C. O.

The illustrator would like to thank the models who were used, most especially Mike Shaver
and Amanda Sartor as John and Abigail Adams, Ryan Pritchett and Rachel Quimby as
assorted young characters, and Jessica Silks for modeling and for her help with photography.

ALADDIN PAPERBACKS

An imprint of Simon & Schuster Children's Publishing Division

1230 Avenue of the Americas, New York, NY 10020

Text copyright © 2005 by Deborah Hopkinson

Illustrations copyright © 2005 by Craig Orback

All rights reserved, including the right of reproduction in whole or in part in any form.

ALADDIN PAPERBACKS, READY-TO-READ, and colophon are registered trademarks of
Simon & Schuster, Inc.

Designed by Lisa Vega

The text of this book was set in CenturyOldst BT.

Manufactured in the United States of America

First Aladdin Paperbacks edition January 2005

2 4 6 8 10 9 7 5 3 1

The Library of Congress has cataloged the library edition as follows:

Hopkinson, Deborah.

John Adams speaks for freedom / by Deborah Hopkinson ;
illustrated by Craig Orback.—1st Aladdin Paperbacks ed.

p. cm.—(Ready-to-read stories of famous Americans)

ISBN 0-689-86907-X (Aladdin pbk.)—ISBN 0-689-86908-8 (lib. ed.)

1. Adams, John, 1735–1826—Juvenile literature. 2. Presidents—United States—
Biography—Juvenile literature. I. Orback, Craig. II. Title. III. Series.

E322.H56 2005 973.4'4'092—dc22 2004008651

CHAPTER 1
FARM BOY

"The Revolution was in the minds and hearts of the people." —*John Adams*

John Adams lived with his family on a peaceful farm. He hated to leave home. But he did.

More than anything, John loved America. He never wanted to cross the seas to live in a faraway country. But he did.

John Adams traveled far and wide for one reason: to speak for freedom. John was a patriot and our second president. This is his story.

John Adams was born in Braintree, Massachusetts. His family had lived in this quiet village for a hundred years.

As a boy, John loved to roam the woods and fields. He walked along the sandy beaches.

John liked to fly kites and play with marbles. He loved making toy boats and sailing them in Fresh Brook.

John loved books just as much as he loved the outdoors. When he was fifteen, he took a test to enter Harvard University in Boston. To his delight, he passed! John's father sold ten acres of land to help pay for college.

John had a sharp mind and loved to talk. After college he studied the law. He was ready to make his way in the world.

John worked hard at being a lawyer. He rode his horse all over New England to speak in court. But although John did well, he often felt lonely. Then he met Abigail Smith.

Abigail was bright and curious. Like John, she was interested in everything that went on in America. She wasn't afraid to speak her mind either. In fact, Abigail liked to talk almost as much as John did.

John and Abigail fell deeply in love. Several years later they were married. They moved to a farmhouse next door to where John had been born.

Whenever John was away from home, Abigail wrote many letters to him.

Abigail began each letter the same way. She called John "My Dearest Friend." And he was.

CHAPTER 2
OFF TO PHILADELPHIA

John and Abigail were happy together. Soon they had four children. Their names were Abigail (called "Nabby"), John Quincy, Charles, and Thomas. Another girl, Susanna, died before she was two.

John and Abigail's home was peaceful. But in America things were not peaceful at all. John and Abigail knew they had to help.

At this time there were thirteen colonies in America. The colonies were part of a country called Great Britain. George III was the king.

King George wanted more money from the colonies. He made Americans pay a tax each time they bought paper, tea, or other things. The king also sent soldiers to Boston to keep order.

People in the colonies became angry about the taxes and the soldiers.

They began to wonder: Should the colonies stay part of Great Britain? Or should they break away and form a new country?

To decide what to do, the colonies formed the Continental Congress. The colony of Massachusetts sent five men to Congress. John was one of them.

One cold winter day in 1776, John Adams kissed Abigail and the children good-bye. He got on his horse and began the long ride to Philadelphia.

John loved his family very much and didn't want to leave them. But John loved America, too. He wanted to help America become a free country.

John said, "Swim or sink, live or die, I am with my country."

CHAPTER 3
JOHN ADAMS SPEAKS FOR FREEDOM

John Adams knew this was an important time for America. He also knew that not everyone in the Continental Congress wanted to break away from Great Britain.

Some people were afraid of a war. They didn't think the colonies could win against such a powerful country. They weren't ready to take the steps toward freedom.

For months John and the other men in Congress argued about what to do. At last, in June of 1776, Thomas Jefferson of Virginia was asked to draft a statement—the Declaration of Independence.

By July the Congress was ready to vote. Should the thirteen colonies of America declare themselves a free and independent country?

John knew there would be no going back. To accept the Declaration of Independence would mean war with Great Britain. This would be the greatest debate of all.

John Dickinson from Pennsylvania spoke first. He said America was too weak to win a long war. He believed America should stay with Great Britain.

John Dickinson sat down. Outside, a summer storm began. The rain hit the windows. The thunder roared.

But inside the men were quiet. Would no one speak for freedom?

Suddenly John Adams leaped to his feet. All eyes turned toward him.

No one knows the exact words John Adams said that day.

We do know that John spoke directly from his heart.

"He moved us from our seats," said Thomas Jefferson.

John spoke for two hours. The whole debate lasted for nine hours.

Finally, on July 4, 1776, the Congress voted to pass the Declaration of Independence.

Three days later the Declaration was read aloud to a cheering crowd. All over the city, bells chimed.

The American Revolution had begun. And John Adams had helped make it happen.

CHAPTER 4
DANGER AT SEA!

America couldn't win the war alone. So Congress asked John to go to France on a secret mission to ask for help.

One snowy night John and his ten-year-old son, John Quincy, waited by the shore. Sailors came in a small boat and rowed them out to a ship, called the *Boston*.

"The wind was very high, and the sea very rough," John wrote.

At first all went well. Then one night a fierce storm struck. The wind howled. The waves looked as high as mountains. *Crack!* As John looked up he saw a bolt of lightning hit the mainmast. The mast split! The ship rolled and trembled.

But John and his brave young son stayed calm. And soon the storm passed.

After six weeks the *Boston* landed safely in France. John had important work to do.

America fought for a long time to become a free country. John spent most of the war in France. He asked other countries to help America.

And in 1783 John Adams was one of three men who signed the peace treaty with Great Britain.

America was a free country at last!

CHAPTER 5
A TRUE PATRIOT

John Adams was glad he could help his new country be born.

John spent ten years in Europe serving his country. When the children were grown, Abigail joined him there.

When John and Abigail came home at last in 1788, a large crowd welcomed them. Church bells rang. People eagerly thanked John for all he had done.

John Adams was ready to stay home on his farm. But once again his country needed him.

When George Washington was chosen to be the first president, John became the vice president.

John was vice president for eight years. Then, in 1797, he became the second president of the United States.

After four years John and Abigail went home. Abigail died in 1818, but John lived to see his son, John Quincy, become president too.

John hoped to live long enough to see America celebrate fifty years of independence.

And he did.

John Adams, who always spoke for freedom, died on Independence Day, July 4, 1826. He had served his country long and well.

Here is a timeline of the life of John Adams:

1735   Born October 30 in Braintree, Massachusetts

1755   Graduates from Harvard University

1764   Marries Abigail Smith on October 25

1765   John and Abigail's first child, "Nabby," is born

1767   John and Abigail's son John Quincy is born

1774   John chosen as a delegate to the First Continental Congress

1776   American colonies declare independence from Great Britain

1778   John and ten-year-old John Quincy sail to France

1783   Signs the Treaty of Paris ending the American Revolution

1788   Returns home from duties in Europe

1789   Becomes first vice president of the United States under George Washington

1797   Becomes second president of the United States

1801   Thomas Jefferson becomes third president

1818   Abigail Adams dies on October 28

1825   John's son John Quincy becomes sixth president of the United States

1826   John Adams and Thomas Jefferson both die on July 4